JIM DOWNING

MEDITATION

THE BIBLE TELLS YOU HOW

NAVPRESS

A MINISTRY OF THE NAVIGATORS

P.O. Box 6000, Colorado Springs, Colorado 80934

The Navigators is an international, evangelical Christian organization. Jesus Christ gave His followers the Great Commission to go and make disciples (Matthew 28:19). The aim of The Navigators is to help fulfill that commission by multiplying laborers for Christ in every nation.

NavPress is the publishing ministry of The Navigators. NavPress publications are tools to help Christians grow. Although publications alone cannot make disciples or change lives, they can help believers learn biblical discipleship, and apply what they learn to their lives and ministries.

© 1976 by The Navigators
All rights reserved, including translation
Library of Congress Catalog Card Number: 76-24064
ISBN: 0-89109-422-9
14225/250

Sixth printing, 1980

Unless otherwise identified, Scripture quotations are from the *New American Standard Bible*, © 1960, 1962, 1963, 1968, 1971, 1972, 1973, 1975 by The Lockman Foundation. Other versions quoted are the *King James Version* (KJV); *The Living Bible* (LB), © 1971 by Tyndale House Publishers, Wheaton, Illinois; and *The New Testament in Modern English, Revised Edition* by J. B. Phillips (PH), © 1958, 1960, 1972 by J.B. Phillips, published by The Macmillan Company, New York and Collins Publishers, London.

Printed in the United States of America

C
CONTENTS

To Morena
my beloved wife

AUTHOR

Jim Downing is responsible for the Navigator ministry in Europe, the Middle East, and Africa. He joined the staff in 1956 after twenty-four years of service in the United States Navy.

Jim enlisted in 1932 after graduating from high school. When World War II broke out, he was stationed aboard the battleship *West Virginia* in Pearl Harbor. He survived the December 7 attack and went on to serve on numerous other ships during his distinguished career. Reaching officer rank, he later commanded the USS *Patapsco* during the Korean War.

As a speaker, Jim has the rare ability to grasp Bible truths and communicate their applications to everyday life. He travels extensively in his responsibilities, visiting and ministering to people on every continent of the world.

FOREWORD

This book points the way to islands of calm in a world that moves all around us like waves of a restless sea. Jim Downing enlivens his teaching with illustrations of an almost mystical quality. Yet he is an intensely practical man in day-to-day touch with reality where he must make tough decisions. In all his relationships I see him continually showing the compassion and selfless consideration for others that are obvious effects of his own close touch with God.

When I was gathering material for the book *Daws,* I found the name Jim Downing prominent throughout the formative years of The Navigators. Dawson Trotman came to rely on him as a shipboard leader of the sailors who witnessed for Christ in the pre-World War II United States Navy.

I met Jim years later when he was skipper of one of those Navy vessels. As Jim's Navy career was ending, Dawson urged him to join The Navigators staff full time. Jim traveled to Schroon Lake in upstate New York to see Daws at a Navigator conference and accept his invitation. He found that Daws had drowned a few hours earlier.

Jim has filled a strategic place at Navigator headquarters since 1956. In spite of his heavy administrative load, he is much in demand as a conference speaker. He often speaks on the subject of meditation and communion with God and now for the first time has committed this vital material to print.

Jim truly lives his message. Thus the paths to God he describes in this book are not theoretical but paths well-worn by his own feet through years of meaningful Christian living. Walk them with him, and you will find your life richer for it.

BETTY LEE SKINNER

I

INTRODUCTION

An Oriental fable tells of three horsemen who were traveling through the desert at night. Unexpectedly they were confronted by a mysterious person. The stranger told them that they would soon cross the dry bed of a stream.

"When you arrive there," he declared, "get off your horses and fill your pockets and saddle bags from the river bed. At sunrise examine the stones you have picked up. You will be both glad and sorry."

As the man predicted, the travelers came to a dry stream bed. In a spirit of adventure they put a few of the many stones they found scattered about into their pockets. At sunrise the next day they examined the pebbles they had picked up. To their great astonishment they found the stones had been transformed into diamonds, rubies, emeralds and other precious stones.

Recalling the statement of the stranger in the

desert, they understood what he meant—they were *glad* for the pebbles they had picked up but *sorry* they hadn't taken more.

This lesson is true also in the Christian life. Your walk with God will be enriched as the truths you appropriate from the Bible are transformed into spiritual jewels to add to your spiritual treasure. One of these spiritual jewels is the ability to get going again after a time of being stalled on a spiritual plateau.

One day when I came home for lunch my wife, Morena, greeted me with, "The washing machine isn't working. I turned it on and the tub filled up with water but nothing else happened."

I went down to the basement and suspecting the gremlin causing the problem was hidden behind the washing machine, I started to slide it out from the wall. As I rocked the machine slightly, the agitator started the water swirling and the machine finished its cycle perfectly. I thereupon instructed my wife to "shake" the machine if it happened again.

It did happen again, and a good "shake" was all that was needed to cause the wash cycle to start. But a question persisted in the back of my mind. *What if she shakes the machine and it does not correct the problem?* So I got my tools out and went to work. I discovered that the spring in the float switch was broken. Ordinarily when the proper water level is reached, a float activates an electric switch which stops the incoming water and starts the wash cycle. But with the switch spring broken, no action occurred after the tub

9

was filled till someone shook the machine.

In the Christian life we sometimes fail to function as we should; but if we read the Bible, pray, hear the Word preached or get exhorted by a friend, we may be "shaken" enough spiritually to get back in the cycle. But what happens if none of these shakings work?

The principles in this book will teach you how to appropriate many spiritual jewels, how to get moving again if bogged down, and how to be revitalized spiritually when you have the unwanted experience of coming to a spiritual plateau or a spiritual halt.

While this book is not an exhaustive treatment of the victorious Christian life, those who put into practice the principles presented will be able to turn pebbles of Christian truth into jewels of Christian experience.

1

GOD'S PICTURE OF
A FRUITFUL CHRISTIAN

For every New Testament truth that God presents, He also has given an Old Testament illustration or picture. The picture illuminating that truth is often worth more than the oft-quoted "thousand words."

For example, when Christ was about to tell of His forthcoming crucifixion, He said to Nicodemus, "As Moses lifted up the serpent in the wilderness" (John 3:14; see Numbers 21:5-9). This statement caught Nicodemus' attention by calling to mind a picture of the historical incident he knew so well. When Jesus spoke of Himself as the Good Shepherd, the minds of His Jewish audience must have gone back to David's immortal words on the Lord as his personal Shepherd, the One who takes care of His people (John 10; see Psalm 23).

Many Old Testament incidents, then, were used to illustrate New Testament teachings.

Sharing Christ's Life

The New Testament truth we want to consider is best expressed in the Phillips paraphrase of Jesus' words, "It is the man who shares My life and whose life I share who proves fruitful" (John 15:5, PH). The Old Testament picture of this New Testament truth is found in the words of the Prophet Jeremiah, "Blessed is the man who trusts in the Lord and whose trust is the Lord. For he will be like a tree planted by the water, that extends its roots by a stream and will not fear when the heat comes; but its leaves will be green, and it will not be anxious in a year of drought nor cease to yield fruit" (Jeremiah 17:7, 8).

We want to isolate and examine the three things that Jeremiah talks about. First, the tree in the prophet's statement was faced by the adversities of heat and drought. We don't know how hot it was or how dry it was, but it must really have been dry. Perhaps it had not rained for three years and the temperature was 120° in the shade.

A tongue-in-cheek story out of the American Southwest tells of an incident during a drought. No rain had fallen for three years. Finally the drought was broken, and one of the citizens got caught in the ensuing rainstorm. It was so sudden and so unexpected that he passed out. According to the tale, it took three buckets of sand to revive him. The tree Jeremiah talks about was in the midst of an extended heat and drought wave.

Second, under these adverse climatic conditions an extraordinary phenomenon took place. In spite of the heat and drought, the leaves of the tree remained green and it never missed a fruit-bearing season. This does not seem to have occurred naturally.

The third point is that the tree had a secret, and its secret was that it spread out its roots by the river. The roots of the tree, especially the taproot, maintained contact with the life-giving moisture that the river supplied.

This passage is the Old Testament picture of the New Testament truth of John 15:5. The Old Testament tree, with its taproot drawing nourishment from the river, is a picture of a Christian, the taproot of whose soul is in contact with Jesus Christ, and who is therefore sharing His life and bearing His fruit.

A fruit-bearing Christian has learned how to thrust the taproot of his soul into contact with the divine resources and draw from God the nourishment needed regardless of time, place or circumstances. God, speaking through Isaiah, said, "The remnant [true believers] . . . shall again take root downward and bear fruit upward" (Isaiah 37:31). A fruit-bearing Christian, then, is like a fruit-bearing tree, in that the soul's roots are in contact with Christ, sharing His life and drawing needed nourishment from Him.

What did Christ mean by fruit when He said, "The person who shares My life and whose life I share will prove fruitful"? To discover what fruit is, we need to examine the rings on the stump of a felled tree. These rings are called annual rings and reveal the tree's age. But the tree's rings also reveal other information. The narrow rings were formed in years of drought. When the ring is larger, it indicates that nourishment was ample that year.

This is an important discovery to which there is a spiritual parallel. We hear a great deal about the importance of maintaining priorities these days. This is not a new idea. God established priorities for trees, not in how they use their time, but how they take in nourishment.

Priority number one is that if only a small amount of nourishment is available it is used to sustain the life already in the tree. My office is in a building situated in the foothills of the Colorado Rockies. Outside my window a small evergreen tree is growing out of the side of a rocky cliff. In the many years I have observed it, it doesn't appear to have grown at all. It comes by what nourishment it gets with a great deal of difficulty and all that nourishment is used just to sustain the life that is already there.

The second priority is that when nourishment is available over and beyond the need to sustain life already in the tree, the tree grows in all directions—upward, downward, outward. Hence we notice that some of the annual rings are larger than others.

When the needs for supporting the life already present and the needs for growth have been met, and there is still more nourishment available, the third priority comes into operation. If there is an abundance of nourishment over and above that needed to sustain life and provide growth, it is transformed into fruit. A fruit tree might be considered temperamental if we could attribute personality to a tree. Till the needs for sustaining life already present and providing for growth have been met, it will not bear luscious fruit.

What then is fruit? It is the overflow, the surplus, the excess life of the nourishment taken into the tree over and beyond that needed for life and growth. Fruit is simply *excess life*. Next time you hold an orange or an apple in your hand you can say, "This is excess life which overflowed after the tree's need for nourishment and growth had been met."

Many of us have seen the pathetic sight of a Christian trying to bear fruit. He has been trying through self-effort to work up courage to witness or be consistent in prayer. When we have partaken of the life of Christ in such abundance that our life-sustaining needs are met and our growth needs are met, the overflow of the love of Christ, the life of Christ, turns into fruit.

The Place of Adversity

Throughout history both military and merchant fleets of sailing vessels have been a great factor in the economy and security of maritime nations. The most important structural member of this type of ship was its foremast. The force of the wind against the heavy sail it supported subjected it to heavy strain. In time of greatest need it would sometimes break and jeopardize the ship and its cargo, as well as the lives of the crew members themselves. If the mast proved faulty, a ship-builder's reputation would also suffer.

To guard against such a disaster, enterprising

shipbuilders selected trees located on tops of high hills as potential masts. They would then cut away all surrounding trees which would in any way shield the chosen tree from the force of the wind. In succeeding years as the winds blew from the north, south, east and west, the tree grew stronger and stronger under the opposition of adverse forces. Finally it was ready to become the foremast of a ship.

If it were possible to observe the moisture intake of the tree during these years of maturing, one could observe an upsurge during each windstorm. The friction generated by the bending of the tree produced heat, causing the tree to draw added nourishment. The same would be true when the sun was pouring out its intense heat. Moreover, in the case of a fruit tree, the greatest intake of water would be as the fruit was being formed. In fact, if the naked eye could x-ray the action inside the trunk of the tree during the fruit-bearing season, the upflow of moisture would resemble an upside-down waterfall.

Adversity in our walk with God is part of our maturing process. He allows it to strengthen us and increase our fruit-bearing. The experiences which God allows in our lives call for varying degrees of partaking of Christ's life, and we know He will water us every moment. Adversity, then, is an opportunity for Christians to draw on God's resources just as a tree draws additional nourishment in times of stress. You can be a living illustration of the tree which spread out its roots by the river. Because it did, its leaf stayed green in heat and drought, and it never ceased bearing fruit. This is the goal of the Christian—to be a fruit-bearing disciple of Jesus Christ regardless of the adversities that may come his way.

The Promise

God gives us another picture of how sharing Christ's life is like a tree being nourished. Speaking of His relationship with His people, who are likened to a vineyard, God says, "I, the Lord, am its keeper; I water it every moment . . . guard it night and day" (Isaiah 27:3).

Not many of us maintain our lawns perfectly. Much of the time they are either too wet or too dry. One way to solve the problem would be to invent and install an automatic moisture meter for each clump of grass. Its function would be to turn on the sprinkler each time a molecule of water was needed by a clump of grass. This seems to be a task beyond our accomplishment. But God says to His people, "I water you every moment." The instant you need God's quickening touch, whether it is day or night, He will provide it. He has made provision and He promises He will nourish our souls in any time of need.

The Soul's Powers

The channel through which we share Christ's life is the taproot of the soul, which corresponds to the roots of the tree we have been discussing (see Jeremiah 17:8).

The Psalms give us the key to understanding how we share God's spiritual life. In many of them we listen in on the words and conversation of a person fellowshiping with and worshiping God. In a way it's like eavesdropping. We often find the psalmist speaking directly to God as he says:

- *"O Lord,* how my adversaries have increased!" (Psalm 3:1)
- "Answer me when I call, *O God"* (4:1)
- "Give ear to my words, *O Lord"* (5:1)
- *"O Lord,* do not rebuke me" (6:1)
- *"O Lord my God,* in Thee I have taken refuge" (7:1)
- *"O Lord, our Lord,* how majestic is Thy name in all the earth" (8:1)
- "I will sing praise to Thy name, *O Most High"* (9:2)
- "Why dost Thou stand afar off, *O Lord?"* (10:1)

In his contact with God, the psalmist also speaks of himself as follows:

- *"My soul,* wait in silence for God only" (62:5)
- *"My soul* waits for the Lord" (130:6)
- "To Thee, *O Lord,* I lift up *my soul"* (25:1)

These passages indicate that coming into contact with God involves the soul. What is that immaterial part of man known as the soul? Theologians in general agree as to the soul's principal powers. They are the *mind,* the *affections* and the *will.* Someone has pointed out that with the mind the soul knows, with the affections the soul feels and with the will the soul chooses.

Bringing the soul in contact with God involves the mind, the affections and the will. Scripture has much to say on each of them. Just as the tree draws nourishment to sustain life—for growth and for overflow into fruit—so the taproot of the soul, which includes the mind, the affections and the will, is God's provision for us to share Christ's life, to sustain our spiritual lives and to grow and overflow into Christlike fruit. The whole concept may be illustrated as follows:

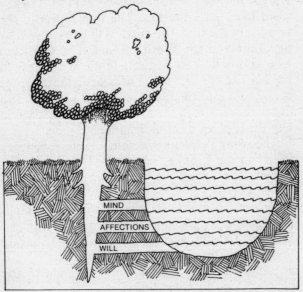

Figure 1

The First Psalm deals with a topic parallel to Jeremiah's. "He [the fruitful believer] will be like a tree firmly planted by streams of water, which yields its fruit in its season, and its leaf does not wither; and in whatever he does, he prospers"

(Psalm 1:3). Several interesting parallels may be seen. In both passages we see a tree planted by the river. It brings forth fruit. Its leaf does not wither.

To this point we have not had a single hint how this illustration may be made a reality in our lives. The psalmist, however, gives us the secret. It is that "his delight is in the law of the Lord, and in His law he *meditates day and night"* (1:2). The key word here is meditation. The first aspect of the taproot of the soul, the mind, is to be exercised by meditation in the Word of God. The Christian who knows how to meditate in the Word of God has learned the first secret of sinking that taproot of the soul into the living resources of Christ and drawing from Him the spiritual inflow needed in any time, place or circumstance.

The second clue for the soul's exercise is again found in the Prophet Jeremiah. The promise is, "Their soul shall be as a watered garden" (Jeremiah 31:12, KJV). The preceding context describes an intimate relationship with God, climaxed by a question: "Who is this that engaged his heart to approach unto Me?" (30:21) Sharing the life of Christ and having Him share ours is accomplished by engaging our hearts with the heart of God in *communion*.

These are two provisions for partaking of God's resources—exercising the mind in meditation, exercising the affections in communion. The third power of the soul is the will. It is exercised in *choosing*. The psalmist commands, "Trust in the Lord, and do good; . . . and verily thou shalt be fed" (Psalm 37:3, KJV). A paraphrase could be, "In time of conflict or testing, choose good; choose to obey. God's response will be to impart spiritual nourishment to you."

When a soul chooses to obey God through the will, God responds by feeding that soul spiritually with Himself. God also promises, "If thou draw out thy soul to the hungry, . . . [the Lord will] satisfy thy soul in drought, . . . and thou shalt be like a watered garden, and like a spring of water, whose waters fail not" (Isaiah 58:10, 11, KJV). This is further verified by the promise that he who chooses to obey and to pour himself out in behalf of others, "shall be watered also himself" (Proverbs 11:25, KJV).

Thus, when the will is exercised in choosing to obey God, the soul is nourished by God Himself. When we choose to reach out in ministering Christ to the needy, both to those with Christ and those who are not experiencing the fullness of Christ, God waters us with divine life. His promise to make our souls a watered garden becomes a reality.

We will explore more detailed teaching of the Word in the succeeding chapters. We will emphasize the *how* of exercising the mind in meditation, the affections in communion and the will in resolution and choosing. In exercising these powers, we will learn the application of the tree's secret. By making contact with God through the taproot of the soul, that is, the mind, the affections and the will, we are nourished, sustained and bear fruit, regardless of the time, place or circumstances.

2

THE MIND AND MEDITATION

Nearly 10,000 thoughts pass in and out of our minds daily. God wants as many of these as possible to be spiritually nourishing. The Scriptures have much to say about the mind and meditation, this first and extremely important part of the taproot of the soul. We must remember that we share Christ's very life as we exercise our minds in meditation on the Word of God.

God clearly commanded the process of meditation. In His commission to Joshua, He said, "This book of the law shall not depart from your mouth, but you shall meditate on it day and night, so that you may be careful to do according to all that is written in it" (Joshua 1:8). Meditation is commended in other parts of the Bible as well:

- "Let the words of my mouth and the meditation of my heart be acceptable in Thy sight, O Lord, my Rock and my Redeemer" (Psalm 19:14)

- "When I remember Thee on my bed, I meditate on Thee in the night watches" (63:6)
- "I will meditate on Thy precepts" (119:15, 78)
- "O how I love Thy law! It is my meditation all the day" (119:97)
- "Thy testimonies are my meditation" (119:99)
- "My eyes anticipate the night watches, that I may meditate on Thy Word" (119:148)
- "His delight is in the law of the Lord, and in His law he meditates day and night" (1:2)

It is evident that God has a great deal to say about meditation, considering it a vital exercise of the minds of His children. It is an important subject in the Scriptures, which tell us specifically what we need to learn to do.

God has given us several avenues through which we may partake of the Word of God. In order to be healthy Christians we need to feed on His Word. Two of the ways we do this are through hearing and reading.

One way we feed on the Word of God is to *hear* it preached and taught. A good pastor, for instance, is responsible to feed his congregation, and he does it through faithful exposition of the Word of God. Nehemiah is an excellent example in that he not only read the law of God distinctly to the people, but gave the sense and caused them to understand (Nehemiah 8:8).

John assures us that the person who *reads* the Word of God is blessed (Revelation 1:3). A young boy who recently moved into a new neighborhood made friends with a boy whose grandmother lived with him. It seemed to the new-comer that every time he saw the elderly woman she was reading her Bible. So he asked his new friend, "Why is she always reading the Bible?"

The grandson replied, "I don't know. Maybe she is boning up for her finals."

We need to feed on the Word of God no matter what our age. The Bible is referred to as bread, meat, milk and honey. What these foods do for us physically, the Word of God does for us spiritually as we read it for ourselves.

We also need to *study* the Word of God in order to be intelligent Christians. There is a big difference between reading and studying. Once, when I was enrolled in a current events class, I looked into a magazine that belonged to one of my fellow-students. It was filled with under-linings, marginal notations, and other evidences of careful study. Any studying results in the systematizing of the subject in a way that can be presented to another person in an orderly manner. Studying also prepares us to pass an exam on the contents of the subject at hand.

The same is true with Bible study. A good Bible study method includes (1) original investigation (do this before reading what others have written about the Bible passage); (2) a written reproduction of the passage in your own words; (3) a personal application; (4) systematic progression (that leads to knowing more and more of the content of the Bible); and (5) it must be pass-on-able (the method must be simple enough to be shared with another person).

In order to be skillful Christians in both living and sharing our faith with others, we need to *memorize* the Word of God.

In my early days as a believer in Christ I knew a Christian woman who was convinced she had a needle lodged in the fleshy part of the palm of her hand. She reported that when she was about to yield to temptation she would feel a sharp pain in her hand. Whether her experience was fact or not, it illustrates an important spiritual point—the Word of God in our hearts (Proverbs 7:3) is used by the Holy Spirit to remind us to resist the onslaughts of temptation.

While trying to persuade his neighbor to yield his life to Christ, a Christian man I knew did not rely on his own wisdom and abilities to answer difficult questions, but always quoted passages of Scripture prefacing them by, "Thus says the Lord . . . " The neighbor finally came to Christ, admitting that because of the authority of the memorized Word of God, "I could no longer argue with God."

Regardless of the method of intake, we need to apply what we find in the Scriptures into our lives. James gives us an excellent illustration of this truth (James 1:22-25). Just as we never look into a mirror without detecting some flaw in our appearance, we never can look into the Word of God without its mirroring some spiritual flaw which, unless attended to, will negatively affect our lives.

Finally, we become fruitful Christians by *meditating* on the Word of God.

The Process of Meditation

Just what is meditation? One of the synonyms given by most regular dictionaries is the word *ruminate.*

Many animals, among which are cattle, sheep, goats, antelope, camels and giraffes, are in a class called ruminant animals. They have four stomachs each, or to be more technical, each has a stomach with four compartments. The first part or the first stomach is called the *rumen.*

The way this particular class of animal goes about the digestive process is not the most elegant by human standards. If you've ever watched a dairy cow eat bluegrass, you will notice that she goes out early in the morning, puts her head down like a mowing machine, and never lifts it until someone disturbs her. She really concentrates on eating.

When I was in the Navy, we had a fellow on board ship who ate rather rapidly. One day one of the men at the table where we sat put an adjustable end-wrench next to his plate. When the rapid eater came in, he picked up the wrench and asked, "What's this for?"

His shipmate replied, "It is to help you bolt down your food."

And that's what the ruminant animal does—just bolts down its food. Then about ten o'clock in the morning, when the sun begins to get hot, the animal lies down in the shade and regurgitates the food out of stomach one, the rumen. This time it chews it thoroughly. The food then goes into stomachs two, three and four. Eventually the digested food is absorbed into the animal's blood stream, and literally becomes part of its life.

A friend of mine, Dr. Hubert Mitchell of the Great Commission Prayer League, spent a number of years in India. He once told us that he was watching a cow lying by a stream ruminating, and was fascinated by her precision. He thought she must have a built-in timer, so he clocked her with his wristwatch and discovered that she would regurgitate a bite of grass, chew it for 55 seconds, swallow it and bring up another. As long as he timed her she never varied one second from the 55. If she had chewed it for 54, she might have missed a little bit of nourishment. If she chewed it for 56, she would have wasted some time and effort.

Rumination and meditation are parallel words. They are synonyms. A cow brings her molars down on her cud, and every time she brings pressure with her teeth, nourishment is forced out of the grass, is mixed with the salivary juices, and goes into her other stomachs. The nourishment she has extracted from her food literally becomes part of her bloodstream.

As we meditate on the Word of God, the life of Jesus Christ flows out of Him, through the Word, and becomes a part of our spiritual bloodstream. The Bible is the primary means by which we share the life of Christ.

A friend of mine once said that he felt our organization, The Navigators, made a fetish out of the Word of God and worshiped it more than we did Christ. In a well-meaning way he said he did not want anything to get between him and Christ, not even the Bible. I certainly agree with his statement; however, the Word of God does not get between the soul and God. It is a door, not a barrier, by which we have contact with Him and share His life. Scripture is quite clear on this. David said, "I will bow down toward Thy holy temple, and give thanks to Thy name for Thy lovingkindness and Thy truth; for Thou hast magnified Thy Word according to all Thy name" (Psalm 138:2).

Two other passages in the Word of God have something to say on this subject. When I was a new Christian, I attended a Bible study at the YMCA in Bremerton, Washington. The teacher was an old veteran of the Brethren Assemblies. When he taught Psalm 40, he suggested that the punctuation in verse seven might not emphasize the most important meaning of the passage, "Then said I, 'Lo, I come; in the volume of the book it is written of Me'" (KJV).

Scholar friends have told me that in the original Hebrew and Greek the inspired Word did not have punctuation. That was supplied in subsequent translations to make the Scripture more readable. (Note for example how various current translations punctuate differently.) Our instructor, a man of many years' experience, felt that the proper emphasis of the passage was brought out when the punctuation was changed, "Lo, I come in the volume of the book," with Jesus Christ speaking prophetically through David. Christ does come into our lives in the volume of the

Book, the Word of God. The only revelation we have of Him is through the Scriptures.

In the 1950s The Navigators had their primary training program at the Glen Eyrie conference grounds in Colorado Springs, Colorado. Part of the training was to arrange for each person in the program to set aside at least a half day each month to be alone with God. To those who had never tried to do this it was a frightening thought. What in the world would they do? A half day alone with God!

Those of us in charge of the program would then give them some orientation, tell them what to take with them into the hills and suggest what they should do. One of the pieces of equipment we recommended very highly, in fact at the top of the list, was to take the Bible. The trainees could very well have gotten out there among the trees and rocks, the hills, the bushes and the clouds, and tried to make contact with God and not have been able to do it. But when we open the Bible, we make contact with Him. He truly does come in the volume of the Book.*

Another illustration of this truth is in the Gospel of John. Christ had just fed a multitude miraculously (John 6:1-14). This was a great experience for His followers. In fact, some of them probably observed that becoming His

---

*For further helpful suggestions on how to spend an extended time with Jesus Christ, see the NavBooklet *How to Spend a Day in Prayer,* by Lorne C. Sanny. You may obtain it from your local Christian bookstore or from NavPress, P.O. Box 1659, Colorado Springs, Colorado 80901.

follower was better than retirement and a social security pension. Whenever they had a need He would rearrange the atomic structure of matter to provide for that need. But Christ was displeased with this response and told His listeners that the bread which He had miraculously provided would not do anything for them spiritually. They cited an Old Testament precedent, "Our fathers ate the manna in the wilderness; as it is written, 'He gave them bread out of heaven to eat'" (6:31). This bread had come down six days a week for 40 years. But it didn't do a great deal for their spiritual lives. So Jesus inferred, "The bread that I miraculously provided for you will not do anything for you spiritually either." He said in effect, "You have to eat and feed on Me. I am the One who gives you spiritual nourishment."

How do we feed on Him? Christ explained that when He said, ". . . the words that I have spoken to you are spirit and are life" (6:63). The Bible, then, rather than being a barrier between us and Christ, is the means that He has provided for His people to share His life.

Just as a ruminant animal extracts nourishment from grass or hay through chewing and transferring it into its bloodstream, so also as we meditate on the Word of God we extract the life of Christ and transfer that life into our spiritual bloodstreams. This is the fulfillment of Jesus' statement, "It is the man who shares My life and whose life I share who proves fruitful" (John 15:5, PH).

The Subconscious in Meditation

The importance of meditation is seen by the commands and promises of God to Joshua and through the psalmist (Joshua 1:8; Psalm 1:3). What a fascinating challenge to actually meditate day and night! Is this an exaggeration for emphasis? Not at all. Are we to take the command literally? Certainly. Is it possible to obey this command? Yes, and we are going to find that it is not only possible to meditate day and night, but meditating in the night is the key to meditating in the daytime. It is the open secret of practical, blessed, hour-by-hour living.

Have you ever had the experience of every muscle in your body going rigid just as you were ready to drop off to sleep? You get stiff all over, seem to leap an inch off the mattress and knock all the blankets off the bed. It happens in a split second, but you are aware that your bodily behavior has been unnatural. Your heart is now beating rapidly and you are short of breath. You wonder, *What has happened? Did my heart stop?*

By the way, have you ever used the expression "go to sleep"? Where do you *go* when you go to sleep? It is commonly recognized that each of us has a conscious mind and a subconscious mind. We don't know a great deal about how they work, but one thing that seems to occur when we go to sleep is that the conscious mind goes off duty. The human body is an intricate mechanism and has to have some organ controlling it even during sleep if the heart is to keep beating, the blood circulating and the lungs pumping air. This job falls to the subconscious mind. One of its responsibilities is to keep the body functioning normally and to sustain life during sleep.

It is widely recognized that one of the greatest problems in human relations is the matter of communication. Any communication that can be missed or misunderstood will be. Thus, it seems that a communication breakdown between the conscious mind and the subconscious mind is possible. The conscious mind thinks that the subconscious knows it is about to leave and will be taking over the control of the bodily functions. But a communication breakdown occurs.

Let's assume that during your waking hours every muscle, nerve fiber and cell of your body is under the command of the conscious mind. Let's assume further that during your sleeping hours these same nerves, muscles and cells are under the control of the subconscious mind. This means that there is an instant in which the conscious relinquishes control to the subconscious.

This seems to be the explanation of the phenomenon described previously—the sudden rigid flexing of the body just before going to sleep. The conscious mind turned over the control of the bodily functions to the subconscious mind, but for some reason the subconscious did not immediately assume control. To its horror the conscious mind suddenly realized that the subconscious was not in control and that tragedy was about to occur. For an instant neither conscious nor subconscious was controlling the bodily life functions.

So the conscious mind called out, "Attention!" and every muscle, nerve and cell in the body responded. Hence the sudden flexing of the muscles, the rapidly beating heart and the stepped-up breathing. Usually, however, the transition is smooth and not noticeable, and you drop off to sleep effortlessly. If the subconscious mind "gets the word," we drift off into a deep sleep, out of the conscious into the subconscious without even being aware that a transfer of responsibilities has taken place.

At the instant the conscious mind turns over control of the body to the subconscious another phenomenon takes place. When the conscious mind relaxes, it relaxes completely; in fact, it empties itself totally. And so the most prominent item in the conscious mind is then transferred to the subconscious. Too often, that which is transferred is in the form of an unsolved problem (we call it worrying).

The response of the subconscious mind to inheriting the unsolved problem is, "What a dirty trick!" The subconscious mind knows full well what its main job is—to rebuild the physical and mental parts of the body completely to their greatest peak of energy and usefulness. It does so by decelerating the heartbeat from a normal 72 beats per minute to 60 or less. Then the amazing process of renewal brings every cell, muscle and nerve in the body to its greatest efficiency. If all goes well, it becomes a common experience for some of us to wake up at three o'clock in the morning so charged up with energy that we cannot stay in bed any longer. We have to get up and start burning energy.

When the conscious mind transfers an unsolved problem to the subconscious, a restless night might be in store. For the subconscious mind to concentrate on a problem it did not want requires energy. And energy must be generated by sugar in the bloodstream. Increased demands for energy call for increased blood circulation, which in turn requires more heartbeats per minute.

This normal function is completely upset when you try to sleep with the worry of unsolved problems on your mind. Instead of relaxing, you toss and turn. It seems as if the subconscious mind gets tired of struggling with the problem and hands it back to the conscious mind. Thus you wake up many times during the night as the problem keeps bouncing back between the conscious and subconscious minds. As you wake up in the middle of the night, the problem which might have been somewhat bearable when you went to sleep becomes unbearable at two in the morning.

The subconscious mind, not being at the peak of efficiency in weighing the facts, gets them distorted. So when you wake up, the facts are distorted and the problem seems even more acute and aggravated than when you tried to go to sleep with it. No wonder that by three o'clock you are *not* filled with energy and ready to get up and start burning it. There has been a sort of tug-of-war throughout the night between the conscious and, the subconscious. So you get up in the morning more exhausted then when you went to bed.

All this came about because of the misuse of the subconscious. There is, however, a legitimate use of the subconscious mind during the hours of sleep.

Meditating Day and Night

Language students have found that if you go over about ten new vocabulary words just before dropping off to sleep, the subconscious mind will start working on them. In the morning, with no further effort, you will know about six of them. So the subconscious does sometimes come through with real efficiency.

I didn't realize it at the time, but in my many years in the Navy aboard ship, the breakfast conversation always seemed to be similar. Usually the subject was the plot of the movie which the crew had seen the night before. Why was it so prominent in their minds? It was because everyone who went to the movie observed the plot and thought about what had taken place, and this was in their subconscious minds as they dropped off to sleep. During sleep the subconscious analyzed the plot and perhaps brought out some features that they hadn't realized. When they woke in the morning, they realized there were several new angles in the plot they hadn't appreciated when they saw the movie. Hence the reason for the breakfast conversation. The subconscious had greatly enhanced the plot and passed it back to the conscious in its amplified state.

It is not God's intention that the subconscious

mind be occupied with movie plots or unsolved problems. Hence the clear command in the Word of God (Joshua 1:8; Psalm 1:3). We are called on to meditate on the Word of God day and night. In order to do so, we must make use of the subconscious. We need to make sure that the last prevailing thought in our conscious minds at the end of the day is some portion of the Word of God.

Dawson Trotman, founder and first president of The Navigators, a good friend and close associate of mine for many years, mastered this principle. In the excellent account of his life and ministry *Daws,* Betty Skinner reports:

> Dawson's love of the unadorned Word also led him unwittingly to apply a principle of meditation that psychologists would later stress as an important influence on the mind—the purposeful use of the subconscious, the theory that the last dominant conscious thought will inevitably simmer in the unconscious mind during sleep. Dawson's habit, on a camping trip or even at home, was to say when conversation ended and lights were out, "All right, H.W.L.W.," after which a passage of Scripture would be quoted without comment as the last word spoken. The H.W.L.W. habit—His Word the Last Word—was popular on early Minute Men trips, but Daws and Lila continued the practice through the years, as did others, as a way to end a day with thoughts fixed on the Lord.*

---

*Betty Skinner, *Daws* (Grand Rapids, Michigan: Zondervan, 1974).

Someone has suggested that we need to give God the night key to our hearts. That night key is the Word of God. Solomon states, "When thou goest, it shall lead thee; when thou sleepest, it shall keep thee; and when thou awakest, it shall talk with thee" (Proverbs 6:22, KJV). This is a summary of the relationships between conscious meditation and subconscious meditation, and of their relation to our daily walk.

- Subconscious meditation—"when you sleep, it [the Word of God] will keep you"
- Conscious meditation—"when you awake, it [the Word of God] will speak to you [on awaking in the morning]"
- Our daily walk—"when you go, it [directions from the Word of God] will lead you"

The first thought you had when you awakened this morning was the last conscious thought you had when you were awake the last time during the night. There is a closed circuit between the consious and the subconscious. The conscious mind passes a thought to the subconscious. When the conscious comes back on duty, the subconscious mind passes the thought back to the conscious. If the last waking thought you have is something from the Word of God, when you wake up in the night it will speak right back to you. That's what the Scriptures say. Furthermore, when you awaken in the morning it will be the most prominent thought in your mind.

An intriguing question then arises: How did God decide when the Scripture was concluded? He must have used many criteria. The psalmist gives us a clue: "The counsel of the Lord stands forever, the plans of His heart from generation to generation" (Psalm 33:11). One of the things God made sure was that every problem and every challenge to which any Christian would ever be subjected was written in the Bible along with its solution and His editorial comment.

God knows exactly what is going to happen to each of us in the next 24 hours. Some place in the Bible He has told us about someone else who had the same experience along with His instruction to us in the experience. God is able to use the Scripture to fortify us for the greatest challenges we're going to have to face in the next 24 hours. As we discover the thoughts He gives us from the Bible and allow the subconscious to meditate on them the night before, we are ready to go forth the next day, prepared for any challenge that might confront us. This is the meaning of the last part of Solomon's statement, "When you go, it shall lead you" (see Proverbs 6:22, KJV). The thought, promise or command with which God fortified us from the Word of God during the night is going to be foremost in our minds during the day to minister to us in time of need.

3

HOW TO GET STARTED
IN MEDITATION

Many Christians practice what is known as the
quiet time, the devotional time, the morning
watch or some similar expression which defines
spending time alone with God. A portion of this
quiet time is to be spent reading the Word of God,
for that is the means by which God speaks to the
Christian.

The Necessity of a Plan
God can speak to us even if we randomly open the
pages of the Bible, but He can lead us to put a little
more thought into deciding on the portion of
Scripture we are going to read in our quiet times.

At one time in my Christian life I used to open
the Bible at random. Somehow most often it
seemed to fall open to Psalm 34. This resulted in
my reading that psalm over and over again. One
day I asked myself, *Why is God always leading me
to the 34th Psalm?* I examined my Bible carefully

and discovered that some of the threads of the binding were broken, so it was the crease in the binding that was leading me to Psalm 34 every time I opened the Bible, not necessarily God.

You may have heard the old story about the person who wanted some random guidance from the Bible. He opened the Word and placed his finger on the first verse that his eyes saw. The passage on which his finger fell stated, "And Judas hanged himself."

He didn't think that was quite the message God had for him that day, so he turned to a new part, closed his eyes, and put his finger down. The selected verse stated, "Go thou and do likewise."

He closed the Good Book and tried again. This time the passage read, "What thou doest, do quickly." He decided that he'd better come up with another method of looking into the Bible for divine direction.

These illustrations show the necessity of having a systematic plan of Bible reading during the quiet time. We must plan in advance the portion of the Bible we are going to read.

The diagram of the clock on page 41 shows the main divisions of our 24-hour period—day and night. Every one of us has exactly the same amount of time. It further shows the two divisions of our lives, night—the hours when we are asleep—and day—our waking hours.

Assuming that you retire at 10:30 P.M. and rise at 6:00 A.M, the shaded area is your time of sleep—night—and the white area your time of being awake—day. Meditating day and night

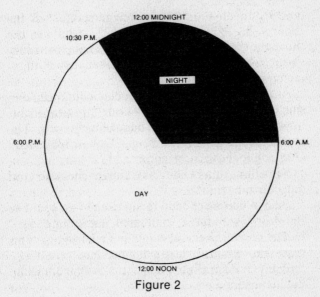

Figure 2

means meditation in all of the 24 hours. And to do that a plan is necessary.

A Workable Plan—Five Psalms a Day

I have used various methods of Bible reading throughout the years, and the one I constantly fall back on is the use of the Psalms. Since there are 150 of them, if we read five every day—every 30th one—we can get through the book once in a month. (We may be late for work, however, the day the 119th Psalm rolls around!)

For the sake of illustration, let us suppose that today is the seventh of the month. My reading for tomorrow will be Psalms 8, 38, 68, 98, and 128 (every 30); on the ninth of the month it will be Psalms 9, 39, 69, 99, and 129. And so on throughout the month. You don't have to think about what you are going to read other than seeing what is tomorrow's date.

As illustrated by the 24-hour clock diagram, the suggestion is that you begin your quiet time not on waking in the morning, but about five minutes *before dropping off to sleep.* As you read, ask God for a thought, a command, a warning, an exhortation, or a praise. Ask Him to speak to you out of your reading.

Before you have read through the five psalms, the Lord will have impressed something particular on your heart and mind. You don't have to read through all five in your presleep reading—only till God speaks to you particularly from what you're reading.

On the seventh of one month I read Psalm 8, and God did not speak to me out of it. I read Psalm 38 and could not see anything in it that He wanted to say to me. Then I read Psalm 68. In that psalm I read, "The Lord . . . daily loadeth us with benefits" (68:19, KJV). The marginal reading in my Bible suggested an alternate reading, "He daily lifts our burdens."

I had been walking around with a burden for four or five days, but had not really realized it. When I came to this passage, I realized, *That's for me! I've been carrying a burden.* God said that He wanted to lift my burdens and then load me up with His benefits. That thought gave me a good night's sleep, and I was thrilled every time I woke up in the night with that thought uppermost in my mind. This enabled me to live on a higher plane the next day than I had been a week before, because that thought sustained me and carried on in my mind throughout the day. It was just what I needed.

Another example may be taken from Psalm 46. You start reading the psalm and you see this statement, "God is our refuge and strength, a very present help in trouble" (verse 1). Immediately you respond with, "Isn't that great! I am going to believe it. During the next 24 hours I am going to appropriate that help, that refuge, that strength of God in any situation that might arise, for that's when I will need the touch of His presence and strength."

Close the Bible—you do not have to read on in this psalm or in Psalms 76, 106 and 136. Make sure no other thought becomes prominent in your thoughts, and drop off to sleep meditating on Psalm 46:1. You should sleep soundly, but if you should awaken during the night, follow the example of the psalmist when he said, "O Lord, I remember Thy name in the night" (Psalm 119:55), and deliberately recall Psalm 46:1 to mind.

This approach continues the application of Solomon's statement, "When thou sleepest, it shall keep thee" (Proverbs 6:22, KJV). If you will discipline yourself to turn your heart and mind to the thought God has given you every time you awaken in the night, and on waking the first thing in the morning, you will discover it has become a part of your life.

A well-known Christian leader has a little different approach to this same principle. A time came after he and his wife had retired for the night that he was through listening before she was through talking. But he encouraged her to continue her part of the conversation with this one restriction—she must quote only Scripture. That assured him that his last waking thought would be on the Word of God.

As previously stated, it is an excellent practice to give God the night key to your heart. This means locking God's Word in your thoughts for the night. If God's Word is locked in, and all other thoughts are locked out, then your subconscious mind must think on what is in that Word.

A word of caution is necessary here. One person with whom I shared this method of putting the Word of God into the subconscious told me the next day that she had a bad night after trying my suggestion. I later discovered that her problem was that she worried about whether or not the process was going to work, so her subconscious was preoccupied with worry as to whether she would be successful. We are not to meditate on meditation, but on the Word of God.

How about trying it *tonight?* If you do, you may be taking a new step in your Christian life. You may be on your way to discovering how you can fulfill the command of God to meditate in His Word day and night and thereby sink the first part of the taproot of your soul—the mind—into the divine resources. Thereby you will draw spiritual life from Christ to prepare you for victory in the spiritual battles that are ahead of you the next day.

No matter what passage you read, God is able to emphasize the message that will satisfy your greatest need for the next 24 hours. Your last waking thought is something from the Word of God. When you wake up in the night, as you start this process, the devil will fight you tooth and nail. He will be right there beside your bed, and when you wake up he will try to slip in a stray thought. Your response should be, "Now wait a minute, that's not what I read out of the Word of God." Then recall the thought you received the night before, and go back to sleep.

Regardless of what approach you use, make sure that your last waking thought is some helpful communication from God. As your subconscious mind takes it up, you enter into the first secret of meditation.

The Morning Quiet Time

Assuming that you go to bed at 10:30 P.M. and get up at 6:00 A.M., and have adopted the suggestions of the previous section, you have fulfilled the first part of the biblical admonition to meditate day and night. What about the period from 6:00 A.M. to 10:30 P.M.? (See the diagram on page 41.) Do you also meditate during that time? The Word answers that question affirmatively when it says, "O how I love Thy law! It is my meditation *all the day*" (Psalm 119:97). Just how do you accomplish that?

Referring to Solomon's statement again,

"When thou awakest, it shall talk with thee" (Proverbs 6:22, KJV). What shall talk with you? The Word of God that was impressed on your heart and mind before you went to sleep the night before, and which your subconscious mind meditated on throughout the night will talk with you.

So what do you *do* in the morning? You go ahead with your regular reading program, and start reading the five psalms for that calendar date. Instead of looking for a new thought, however, you look for parallel passages or parallel thoughts that will give further light and weight to what God has already given you.

For example, suppose the thought God gave you the night before was from Psalm 31:3, "Thou art my rock and my fortress." As you are reading Psalm 61 in your morning quiet time, you read, "Thou hast been a refuge for me, a tower of strength against the enemy" (verse 3); as you read further in Psalm 91, you find, "I will say to the Lord, 'My refuge and my fortress, My God, in whom I trust!' " (verse 2). These passages build on the thought of the night before, and their composite is a real promise that the Lord will be your refuge and fortress throughout the day. They have been parallel thoughts that have amplified and reinforced what you had claimed the night before.

Has this ever happened to you? You heard the catchy tune of a Christian or secular song and somehow that tune so grabbed you that you just couldn't turn it off? I recall the first time I ever heard two of our staff singing the song "Somebody Put Glue on the Saddle." Not only did it have interesting words, but it has a very unusual tune. I was leaving on a week's vacation the next morning and wanted to do some serious thinking and planning. For a whole week I couldn't do anything constructive because that tune kept playing back from the subconscious to the conscious. Every time I tried to have a serious thought that week, it seemed that my body chemistry would play back the tune "Somebody Put Glue on the Saddle." My week was almost ruined.

Meditation During the Day

There seems to be something about the mind and about body chemistry that causes a thought captured by the conscious mind to be transferred into the subconscious mind. Like a tape recording, it is available to be played back—every little bit of it.

This is what is supposed to happen when you place the Word of God in the subconscious. If everything is just right, it is recorded, and at regular intervals it will start playing back into the conscious mind. When we wake up during the night it speaks to us. When we wake up-the next morning the Holy Spirit plays it back to us. That portion of the Word the Lord gave us the night before becomes our periodic meditation all the next day.

This is not to suggest that it is going to be that easy. We do get preoccupied with what we're doing during the daytime. The devil does try to keep our thoughts from God's Word. If we are on an airplane making an instrument landing, we're going to be very happy if the pilot would just concentrate on the instruments and not try to meditate during that time. That is, we do have other responsibilities during the day. But we can be so preoccupied with what we are doing that we forget to meditate on God's Word when there is time.

The Bible suggests some mechanical helps. The psalmist says, "Seven times a day I praise Thee, because of Thy righteous ordinances" (Psalm 119:164). A great missionary, Adoniram Judson, made practical and literal use of this verse. I understand that he divided the clock in his study into seven divisions during the daylight hours. These divisions were about three hours apart. Every time he looked up at the clock to see what time it was, he'd see dividing marks. As the hands approached one of them, he was reminded to meditate.

This suggests the use of natural checkpoints in the day's routine. One well-known Christian turned his attention to the Lord by using the times of 6:00 A.M., 9:00 A.M., 12:00 NOON, 3:00 P.M., 6:00 P.M. and 9:00 P.M. as times to recall the verses for meditation consciously. For practical purposes it might be better to be more general, as before breakfast, morning coffee break, lunch, afternoon coffee break, when you come home, and after supper.

This does not mean that we restrict our meditation to those times only. It will become most natural for us to recall what God has emphasized to us in every time of need during the day. Without a fresh inflow of the life of Christ we approach spiritual fatigue. But if we can just be reminded to recall the verse and meditate on it a little bit during the day, that is a fresh inflow of His life into ours.

I knew of a bus driver who drove in New York City's Manhattan district. Every tenth street, that is every street that ended in zero—10, 20, 30 and so forth—was a reminder to him to meditate on the Word of God. I once suggested to the cadets at the Air Force Academy, who are pretty regimented in their schedule, that as they go from one class to another, they spend that break meditating in the thought God gave them from the Word of God the night before.

If you want a formula that is sure to succeed (and I speak from experience), try this one. Several years ago I bought an alarm wrist watch. The first thing in the morning I would set the alarm ahead one hour and a half. Let's say the time is seven o'clock. At 8:30 the alarm goes off. As I reach down to shut it off, rewind it and set it an hour and a half ahead, I am reminded to recall and meditate on the verse that God gave me the night before.

It is also good to have an unfulfilled challenge to which to look forward. The psalmist gives us one, "At midnight I shall rise to give thanks to Thee because of Thy righteous ordinances" (Psalm 119:62). Though I have not tried this yet, I am reserving it as a future challenge.

The way I first discovered the power of the

Word during the night hours was a providential "accident." At the time, I was responsible for the finances in our organization. At this point in time the financial outlook was critical. I would lie awake trying to figure out what to do with the next day's problems. The reason I thought about it in the middle of the night was that I went to bed worrying about the problem. During this period of my life I had been memorizing the Book of Ephesians. To relieve myself of worry about finances I started reviewing the first three chapters of the epistle. I cannot ever remember getting through the third chapter in review. The Word of God overpowered the worry, took control, and I was able to go to sleep. Truly the psalmist observed, "He gives His beloved sleep" (see Psalm 127:2). If I had placed the Word of God in my subconscious before going to sleep instead of waiting until the middle of the night, I would have been spared many wakeful hours.

God's intended use for the subconscious during the hours of sleep is for the committed Christian to meditate in the Word of God. What is meditation? We have compared it to a ruminant animal chewing the cud, drawing nourishment from the food and transferring it into the bloodstream. As we meditate on the Word of God we literally receive the life of Jesus Christ and transfer it into our spiritual bloodstream. The technique in meditation we are talking about is the *recall technique.* Simply recall, review and meditate on what God has said.

Why do we want to meditate? So we can share His life and be fruitful. Just as Solomon said, when we sleep the Word will keep us, when we awake it will speak with us, when we go, it will lead us (Proverbs 6:22).

Perhaps you don't want to wait till tonight to get started. Get your Bible right now. Start reading the passage you have reserved for your quiet time tomorrow. Maybe God will give you the thought, command or challenge to meditate on right now. Then, the last thing before you expect to drop off to sleep this evening, fix that thought in your conscious mind again. This may take some cooperation from your husband or wife or from your roommate, but it can be worked out easily. Just have an agreement between you that God's Word will be the last word, and that your last five minutes or so before going to sleep are going to be spent fixing a portion from God's Word in your conscious mind so it will be transferred into the subconscious.

Next morning supplement that thought with others in your quiet time. Then as the need for spiritual nourishment arises throughout the day, the Word will be recalled and in meditation nourishment will be released for your own spiritual strengthening or for sharing with others. As we meditate in the Word, day and night, the first part of the taproot of our souls contacts the divine resources and we are strengthened miraculously by becoming partakers of a God-imparted life. Christ's words become a living reality in each of our lives, "the words that I have spoken to you are spirit and are life" (John 6:63).

The diagram of the 24-hour clock on page 41 summarizes the procedure. Starting just before we expect to drop off to sleep, we meditate on the Word of God. During the night hours the subconscious mind integrates that Word into our total beings. If we wake up in the night, it speaks to us; when we awake in the morning, it speaks to us again; as we go throughout the day, that portion that God has given us from His Word leads us.

It is not only possible, but it is a delight to meditate on the Word day and night. As we do it, we can join the psalmist in declaring, "My meditation of Him shall be sweet; I will be glad in the Lord" (Psalm 104:34, KJV).

THE AFFECTIONS AND
COMMUNION

In sharing Christ's life and having Him share ours, meditation opens the spiritual door to communion. Jesus stated, "It is the [person] who shares My life and whose life I share who proves fruitful" (John 15:5, PH). With the taproot of the soul we make contact with God, who provides spiritual watering through that means. The three branches of that taproot are the mind, the affections (or emotions) and the will.

Life consists of knowing, feeling and choosing, as we exercise our minds, affections and wills. We have already considered in great depth the place of the mind in meditation. Now we want to look at the emotions/affections and their exercise in communion.

What Is Communion?
"I will commune with thee," said God to Moses (Exodus 25:22, KJV). What an amazing statement!

The eternal, unchanging, all-knowing God, creator and sustainer of all there is, clothed in majesty and power, wanted to have communion with mortal man. And centuries later He would say to the Prophet Jeremiah, "Who is this that engaged his heart to approach unto Me?" (Jeremiah 30:21, KJV).

We now come to that fascinating second part of the taproot of the soul—the exercise of the affections in communion with God. The idea of communion between God and man originated with God Himself. He initiated the habitual communion with Adam in the Garden of Eden, and even came seeking that fellowship after Adam had sinned (see Genesis 3:8, 9). And God revealed the very longings of His heart when He said to Moses, "I will commune with thee" (Exodus 25:22, KJV).

My wife, Morena, has a ministry with quite a number of women, and so spends much of her time talking on the telephone. I can tell by watching her whether or not she is enjoying the conversation. If she is listening to a telephone sales pitch, occasionally saying, "Uh huh," or making up a shopping list, I know she isn't really communing. But if she is speaking with one of her friends, she listens intently. She becomes animated and speaks up enthusiastically. What the person at the other end of the line is sharing of her life and problems is of intense interest to Morena. It is obvious that this is a reciprocal experience, as what she is saying is eagerly being received on the other end. Sometimes the exchange is so intense I think someone is going to crawl out of the receiver, or Morena is going to crawl into the transmitter.

What has occurred is two-way communication. For a working definition from that illustration, we might say that communion is the alternating impact of two personalities communicating and integrating their very lives into that of the other person. It is fellowship at the highest level. It produces a mutually pleasant result. It is communion on the human plane.

The best description of communion in the Bible is found in God's conversation with the Prophet Jeremiah. God promises that they who meet certain conditions (Jeremiah 30:21) will have their souls watered like a garden (31:12). The condition is expressed in the form of a question, "Who is this that engaged his heart to approach unto Me?" (30:21) Communion, then, is engaging our hearts with the heart of God. The result of that communion is that our soul is watered (31:12). As we exercise the first part of the taproot of the soul, the mind, in meditation, our souls are watered. Now we find that in communion our souls are watered also as we literally share the life of Christ in close fellowship with Him.

Communion, then, is a two-way communication, an alternating impact of two personalities where we listen intently and then share intently with the other person; there is an actual sharing of lives involved. This is what God wanted to do when He said to Moses, "I want to commune with you." It was God's idea; it was His desire, not Moses'.

The Pattern for Communion

God gave Moses a pattern to follow in order for men to commune with Him. The New Testament explanation of this pattern is in the statement, "Christ did not enter a holy place made with hands, a mere copy of the true one, but into heaven itself, now to appear in the presence of God for us" (Hebrews 9:24). The pattern which God gave to Moses in the wilderness was the Old Testament means of communion between God and His people when God Himself inhabited the Old Testament tabernacle. In the New Testament we find, according to the writer to the Hebrews, that Christ is in heaven. The pattern for communing with Him is the same as that which He gave to Moses in the Old Testament.

It is from a pattern God showed men in the Old Testament that we derive our guidance for communing with Christ. What was first inaugurated in the tabernacle in the wilderness was later duplicated in the temple. These are prototypes of the way a Christian is to commune with Jesus Christ who is now in heaven. In the next chapter we are going to discuss 12 steps involved in communion with God. We are not saying that there is a mechanical, structured way to commune with God; we are simply outlining these 12 steps as they seem to be suggested by the tabernacle. Each person desiring to commune with God can decide which principles apply to his or her particular situation.

In the diagram on page 57 we have a representation of the tabernacle. The whole complex con-

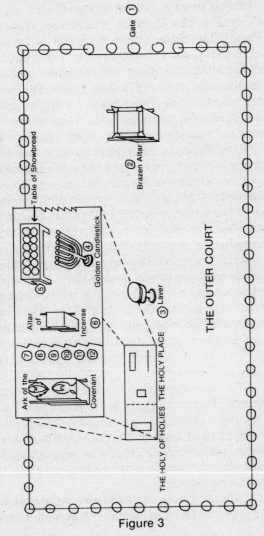

THE TABERNACLE AND ITS FURNITURE

Gate ①

Brazen Altar ②

Table of Showbread

Golden Candlestick ④

③ Laver

Altar of Incense ⑥

⑤

Ark of the Covenant

⑦ ⑧ ⑨ ⑩ ⑪ ⑫

THE HOLY OF HOLIES   THE HOLY PLACE

THE OUTER COURT

Figure 3

sisted of three parts, the Outer Court, the Holy Place and the Holy of Holies (or Most Holy Place). The Outer Court, 50 × 100 cubits (about 75′ × 150′), was enclosed by a curtain of skins with a 20-cubit (30′) door on the east side. Upon entering the gate, the first item to be seen was the brazen altar of sacrifice; beyond it in the court was the laver for washing. Then came the next enclosure, containing the Holy Place and the Holy of Holies, a completely covered tent 10 × 30 cubits (15′ × 45′), with the door again facing east.

Three articles of furniture composed the Holy Place, 10 × 20 cubits in size (15′ × 30′). At the left, as you entered, was the golden candlestand (or lampholder) with seven golden candlesticks (or lamps) on it (also called the Menora); to the right was the Table of Showbread with 12 loaves of unleavened bread on it; straight ahead was the golden Altar of Incense, from which a fragrant odor rose heavenward. Behind the altar was a heavy curtain, the veil, beyond which only the high priest could go, and then only once a year on the Day of Atonement. Beyond the veil was the Holy of Holies.

This last chamber, 10 cubits by 10 cubits square, had one item in it—the Ark of the Covenant, in which were placed Aaron's rod that budded, the tables of the Ten Commandments and a pot of manna. Here the very presence of God abided. Here is where God invited Moses to commune with Him.

From the Book of Exodus we learn that when the tabernacle had been completed, a cloud covered the tent of the congregation, and the glory of God filled the tabernacle (Exodus 40:33, 34). God Himself moved into this tabernacle where He was available to commune with those He ordained should approach Him. We are told that later on because of the disobedience of His people He "forsook the tabernacle" (Psalm 78:60, KJV). But the point is that when He was in the tabernacle and the people could commune with Him, there was a pattern to be followed.

We want to explore this pattern for principles we can apply today. What we are going to do is take a mental journey through the tabernacle in the same way that an Old Testament communicant (a priest delegated with that responsibility) took a physical journey from outside the gate into the very presence of God.

Preparation for Communion

Where is God? We believe that He is not only omniscient (He knows all things), but that He is omnipresent (He is everywhere) as well. In the Old Testament He chose to dwell in the tabernacle, but now He is available to be communed with by men everywhere. David stated, "The Lord is in His holy temple, the Lord's throne is in heaven" (Psalm 11:4). As Stephen was about to enter God's presence, we are told that "being full of the Holy Spirit, he gazed intently into heaven and saw the glory of God, and Jesus standing at the right hand of God" (Acts 7:55). And Habakkuk cried, "The Lord is in His holy temple, Let all the earth be silent before Him" (Habakkuk 2:20).

You do not rush into God's presence. Preparation is needed here just as it is necessary for meditation in the Word of God. In past centuries kings generally allowed only two persons to have unlimited access to them. One was the son who was the heir, the prince, and the other was the jester, the court fool. There was a big difference in the manner in which they entered the presence of the king. The prince showed a respectful restraint and prepared carefully for his time with his father. His approach into his father's presence showed his consideration for his father's position, and respect for the one whom he highly honored.

Not so with the fool. He was too preoccupied with his own lighthearted approach to life to honor the greatness of the king's position. He played his part well—he was the fool. We do not need to rush into the presence of God.

As you are about to commune with God, close your heart and mind to the things of this life and remember that God is on the throne, that He is in His holy temple. From His throne in heaven God is not only administrating the affairs of the universe, but He is attentive to the approach of one of His worshipers, one who responds to His invitation to commune with Him.

To the prepared heart, God is near. The psalmist cried, "Thou art near, O Lord" (Psalm 119:151). As you kneel before God, your Maker and your Saviour, time and space dissolve away, and you are in His very presence before His throne.

5

HOW TO HAVE
COMMUNION WITH GOD

How do we begin our communion with God? With careful preparation (see last chapter), and by going on a reverent journey mentally through the tabernacle. The holy place made with hands brings us back to the pattern God revealed to Moses.

In this pattern there are meanings which are profound for the most diligent seeker. Yet the pattern of approach to God is so simple that the humblest believer can appropriate it. Let us learn the revealed secret from God's pattern as we follow the steps through the tabernacle. (The diagram on page 57 will help us visualize where we are and where we are going.)

Step One: Thanksgiving
We notice from the diagram that the first step begins outside the gate. Scripture tells us that Jesus suffered "outside the gate" (Hebrews 13:12).

This was a fulfillment of the Old Testament sacrifice which a communicant must offer before approaching God. Our suggestion for step one is that we pause in our mental journey outside the gate and *thank* our heavenly Father that He sent Jesus Christ to die for us outside the gates of Jerusalem. This places our approach to God in proper perspective as we realize that it is only because Jesus Christ died for us that we have the right to come into God's presence.

Step Two: Acknowledgment

The Old Testament communicant placed his sacrifice on the brazen altar. Christ became that sacrifice and "we have been sanctified through the offering of the body of Jesus Christ once for all" (Hebrews 10:10). Step two is to tell God that as we approach Him, it is not on the basis of what we have done or haven't done, not on the basis of what we are going to do or not going to do, not on the basis of what we are or are not, but we acknowledge that we can approach Him only on the basis and on the merits of what Jesus Christ has done. As the priest in the Old Testament placed the communicant's sacrifice on the brazen altar, so we mentally present Jesus Christ as our sacrifice and offering, which has opened the way for us to come into God's presence.

Step Three: Confession

The next item in the court of the tabernacle was the laver filled with water. Practically, this was for the priest to cleanse himself from the defilement he may have experienced in offering the sacrifice. In our mental journey, step three is to remind us that God has given us a laver for cleansing. The Bible says, "If we confess our sins, He is faithful and righteous to forgive us our sins and to cleanse us from all unrighteousness" (I John 1:9). We also need to take note of this statement, "He who conceals his transgressions will not prosper, but he who confesses and forsakes them will find compassion" (Proverbs 28:13). In step three we approach God confessing our sins and forsaking in our hearts and intents any sins which have defiled us since we last came into His presence, so that they may be placed under the blood of Jesus.

Step Four: Thanks for Light

The next part of the tabernacle was known as the holy place, and had no windows. No natural light could get in as it was covered on all sides and the top by the skins of animals. As we proceed into the holy place, we notice a candlestand with seven candlesticks on the left. This may remind the present-day communicant of a number of things. One might be the words of Jesus, when He said, "I am the light of the world" (John 8:12). Another might be, "If any of you lacks wisdom, let him ask of God, who gives to all men generously and without reproach, and it will be given to him" (James 1:5). Our fourth step is to thank God audibly that all the light and wisdom we need on the problems for today and the future are available from Him, and we thank Him for it.

Step Five: Thanks for Strength

As we look across to the right side of the holy place, we notice a table of showbread. It was placed there to show that all provision is from God. We are told that bread strengthens man's heart (Psalm 104:15). We are also told to "be of good courage and He shall strengthen thine heart" (Psalm 27:14, KJV). Our fifth step is to thank God for His provision of all the strength that we are going to need for today. The symbolism of the bread for physical strength is parallel to the spiritual strength available to us if we want to claim it.

Step Six: Prayers

The next item in the holy place is the most fascinating. It is the golden altar of incense. Throughout the day a fragrant odor came out of the holy place from the altar of incense. This symbolizes the truth that our presence before God and our approaching Him in communion is a sweet fragrance to Him. John tells us that the prayers of the saints are like incense to God (Revelation 8:4). What a privilege it is for a redeemed sinner to be able to delight the heart of God through prayer. In our sixth step we are to tell God that we thank Him for the privilege of delighting His heart with our prayers and presence as we come to Him.

Many people think too much about what *they* can get out of their quiet times. But the main question here is what is God's side to the quiet time? The altar of incense tells us. When we miss our daily appointment with Him, He is disappointed. Our prayers and our presence are a fragrance to Him.

Step Seven: Worship and Adoration

We note in the diagram that the next part of the tabernacle is the Holy of Holies. It is separated from the other part of the tabernacle by a thick curtain. During the Old Testament days only the high priest could go behind the veil, and that was once a year, on the Day of Atonement (Hebrews 9:7).

We recall that on the day of crucifixion this heavy veil of the temple was torn in two from top to bottom (see Matthew 27:51). The Holy Spirit's explanation of that event is that the way into the holiest of all was now available to every Christian (Hebrews 9:8). So as the Old Testament saint faced the curtain, we face open space, being able to go directly into the presence of God and to commune with Him.

As we walk through the rent curtain and approach a step closer to the very presence of God Himself in our mental journey, our seventh step is worship and adoration. Alfred Gibbs has pointed out that as prayer is the occupation of the heart with needs, and praise the occupation of the heart with blessings, so worship is the occupation of the heart with God Himself. (Prayer and praise do become parts of worship as well.) At this point in our mental journey we want our hearts to be occupied with the greatness of the person of God, and the greatness of all His works. "O Lord my

God, Thou art very great; Thou art clothed with splendor and majesty" (Psalm 104:1; see also I Chronicles 29:11-13).

David commands, "Give unto the Lord the glory due unto His name; worship the Lord in the beauty of holiness" (Psalm 29:2, KJV). How can a human being give glory to God? Let's consider this further. Glory may be defined as displayed excellence or excellence on display. We are told in the Psalms that the glory of a young man is his youth, which seems to refer to his athletic abilities.

Do you know a famous athlete, specifically a football player? Suppose you are watching a football game and see your favorite athletic hero give a sterling performance. As you meet him afterwards, you can't help slapping him on the back, putting your arms around him and saying something like, "It was spectacular the way you caught that pass, then evaded this tackler, stiff-armed that one, ran over this one, got through the last tackle, over the goal line and scored that great touchdown." As you rehearse in his presence what he did, you cannot *add* to his person or to his performance. You cannot take away from his person or his performance. But as you praise his deeds, you are giving glory to him.

We need to rehearse in God's presence what we think about the greatness of His Person and the wonder and greatness of all His works. We might open with, "O Lord my God, Thou art very great; Thou art clothed with splendor and majesty" (Psalm 104:1). Note how personal this approach is, "O Lord *my* God!" Or we might join the heavenly throng and say, "Worthy art Thou, our Lord and our God, to receive glory and honor and power; for Thou didst create all things, and because of Thy will they existed, and were created" (Revelation 4:11). Tell the Lord that He is great, that you praise Him for His greatness and thank Him for being who He is (I Chronicles 29:11-13).To avoid formalism, variety is needed. The adjectives we employ in worshiping God must be those we speak from the heart, based not only on our personal knowledge, but coming out of our personal experience with God. The Scriptures abound with descriptions that can serve as suggestions to us. A few of these are given in Psalm 145, which is a psalm of pure praise to God:

- "On the *glorious splendor of Thy majesty,* and on *Thy wonderful works,* I will meditate" (verse 5)
- "I will tell of *Thy greatness"* (verse 6)
- "They [change it to 'I'] shall eagerly utter the memory of *Thine abundant goodness"* (verse 7)
- "The Lord is *gracious and merciful; slow to anger and great in lovingkindness"* (verse 8)
- "The Lord is *good to all,* and *His mercies are over all His works"* (verse 9)
- "They [make it 'I' again] shall speak of *the glory of Thy kingdom,* and talk of *Thy power"* (verse 11)
- " . . . *Thy mighty acts,* and *the glory of the majesty of Thy kingdom"* (verse 12)

As you read worshipfully through this psalm,

underline all the references to the character of God for which you want to extol Him and personalize them. Another group of suggestions may be found in Psalm 36:

- "*Thy lovingkindness,* O Lord, extends to the heavens" (verse 5a)
- "*Thy faithfulness* reaches to the skies" (verse 5b)
- "*Thy righteousness* is like the mighty mountains" (verse 6a)
- "*Thy judgments* are like a great deep" (verse 6b)
- "O Lord, *Thou preservest* man and beast" (verse 6c)
- "How precious is *Thy lovingkindness,* O God!" (verse 7a)
- "And the children of men take refuge in *the shadow of Thy wings*" (verse 7b)
- "They drink their fill of *the abundance of Thy house*" (verse 8a)
- "And Thou dost give them to drink of *the river of Thy delights*" (verse 8b)
- "For with Thee is *the fountain of life*" (verse 9a)
- "In *Thy light* we see light" (verse 9b)

As you read the Scriptures day by day, be alert for passages which will help you express in your own words your adoration for the Lord. Make this adoration an increasingly meaningful part of your communion as you occupy your heart with God Himself in worship. This is our up-to-date application of the Old Testament communicant's step seven.

Step Eight: Expression of Love

Our next step is suggested by David's heartfelt expression, "I love Thee, O Lord, my strength" (Psalm 18:1). We ought to express our love for God vocally. This may not be easy to do, particularly for those with strong masculine characteristics, but we are commanded in Scripture to tell Him that we love Him. A Dutch translation of that psalm reads, "I love Thee heartily, O Lord," and David was as masculine as you can get. Another psalmist stated, "I love the Lord, because He hears my voice and my supplications" (Psalm 116:1). David exhorts, "O love the Lord, all you His godly ones!" (Psalm 31:23)

The New Testament clearly shows this in the great reciprocal love section given us by John (I John 4:7-21), with the highpoint being, "We love, because He first loved us" (verse 19). Wherever there is a paternal family relationship or a marital union, God has made us so that love needs to be verbally expressed, as well as backed up by actions. God intends that our response to Him be on the same basis.

In order to regiment my own mind, I like to go through the last week of our Lord's life on earth as a reminder of what I need to tell Him I love Him for.

As one approach, follow the Gospel of John from Jesus' Triumphal Entry to His resurrection appearances to the eleven disciples, by either using an open Bible or by mental recollection. Set your heart on these events in our Lord's last days on earth and tell Him you love Him because of who He is and what He has done.

- John 12—"I love You for Your humility in the Triumphal Entry!"
- John 13—"I love You for the Servant You were in washing the disciples' feet!"
- John 14—"I love You as I reflect on the mansions You have gone to prepare for me!"
- John 15—"I love You because of the vine and branch relationship we have through which I am enabled to share Your life!"
- John 16—"I love You because of the power of the Holy Spirit whom You have sent into my life!"
- John 17—"I love You because You included me and prayed for me in that great High Priestly prayer of Yours!"
- John 18—"I love You for the great agony You underwent for me in the Garden of Gethsemane!"
- John 19—"I love You for Your supreme sacrifice for me on the cross!"
- John 20—"I love You for the power of Your resurrection that assures me of mine!"
- John 21—"I love You for the fellowship that You have and enjoy with Your people, of whom I am part!"

These are merely some suggestions on how you can express your love for the Saviour. Everyone who would commune with God must find his own way of doing this step of expresssing his love for Him. But as you engage your heart with the heart of God and recognize the union of your soul with

His life, He in turn gives you life from Himself at any time, in any place and any circumstances.

Step Nine: Pure Praise

This step fulfills the command of the psalmist in which we are told, "Enter His gates with thanksgiving, and His courts with praise. Give thanks to Him; bless His name" (Psalm 100:4). At this point we need to reflect on something which is very important. Is God more interested in hearing us speak with Him about what He has done or what He has not yet done? When we give praise and thanks we are speaking with Him about what He has *already* done. I believe that the Scripture clearly indicates, just by fact of the number of times mentioned, that God is more interested in having us speak with Him about the things He has *already* done than what He has not done. This is praise; this is the occupation of the heart with blessings God has already bestowed. According to the biographer of the great missionary, John Hyde, "Praying" Hyde felt that whenever his prayers were hindered it was because of the lack of praise. In occupying our hearts with blessings through praise we place our relationship with God in proper perspective. The hymn writer suggests to us, "Thou art coming to a King / Great petitions to Him bring." We cannot bring worthy petitions in prayer unless we have first offered sufficient praise.

This is well illustrated by an experience Emperor Napoleon had after one of his conquests. One of the recently conquered people came to Napoleon with a very unusual request. From the record we have it seems that this newly conquered man asked Napoleon to place into his jurisdiction a large number of the people and the territory that had been conquered. Napoleon's chief-of-staff thought the request was so outrageous he wouldn't even consider it, but the man did get to see Napoleon. After just a few minutes with him, Napoleon came out of his tent and told his chief-of-staff to give this man everything he had asked for. The chief-of-staff was astounded. He asked Napoleon how in the world he could consider granting such an outlandish request.

Napoleon's reply reportedly was, "He honored me by the magnitude of his request." It seems that Napoleon was saying, "Anyone who thinks I am that great is not going to be let down."

If we are occupying our hearts with praise, we get the greatness of God and His willingness to give into proper perspective. We are not in a position to bring great petitions to God till we have reflected on the greatness of God and thought about the things He has done in the past, and then spent much time in thanksgiving to Him for that which He has already done.

Step Ten: The Very Presence of God

This step brings us to the very heart of our communion with God. In order to approach this main experience which God has for us, we need to consider a vital question. Do you think there is a possibility that you might enter into God's presence literally while having time alone with

Him? That is, that you might die right in the middle of praying to God? Granting that this could happen, here is another question. If this occurred, would you finish the sentence? Everything depends on how real was the sentence you began as you were talking with God.

I like to imagine that when I arrive into God's presence, He may indicate that I am to speak first, so I have a little speech all prepared. The first thing I am going to say is, "Lord, while I was absent from You in the flesh, I often thanked You for saving me. My salvation is the first thing I want to thank You for now, in person."

Then perhaps the Lord will indicate for me to go on. So I'll say, "Lord, do You remember last week when I got in that jam and I prayed to You and You answered? I thanked You then but I want to thank You again now for doing that, in person." I am sure the Lord will respond with, "Yes, I remember that." Then as He indicates that I am to go on, I'll reach back another few days and say, "Lord, do You remember that experience . . . ?" and describe it to Him. I am sure His response will be, "Yes, I remember that very well." This is an illustration of what it means to speak with God about things that are real to me and real to Him. So in this step I speak with Him about *reality,* things real to Him and real to me. And this is the heart of communion.

In his superb classic *Power Through Prayer,* E. M. Bounds tells of the experience of a French Christian, Marquis DeRenty. According to this account, he went into his study one day to spend some time with God; he instructed his servant to call him 30 minutes later. When that time arrived, his servant came in, but just didn't have the heart to disturb him as he observed that DeRenty was in communion with God. Thirty minutes later he came back again; an hour had now elapsed. It was the same thing—he just couldn't bear to disturb Marquis DeRenty. Finally, 90 minutes later, he came in again and told his master that it was time for him to go on to his office. Marquis DeRenty remarked in surprise, "My, but 30 minutes is such a short time when you're in communion with God!"

When we're talking to God about things which are real to Him and real to us, time stands still. I read in the newpaper once that when Albert Einstein first came to America, an enterprising reporter asked him to give his theory of relativity in just a sentence or two. Einstein rose to the occasion and reportedly said, "Let me illustrate relativity. If you have the bad fortune to sit on a hot stove for one minute, it will seem like an hour; but if you have the good fortune to sit next to a very attractive lady for one hour, it will seem like a minute." I don't know just what point Dr. Einstein was trying to bring out, but the lesson I get from this incident is that *time is relative to enjoyment*.

When we are enjoying something, time just slips away; when we are not, it drags. When we are in communion with God, when we are involved in the reality of that communion, time passes unnoticed.

Step Eleven: Petitions

We have noted previously that prayer is the occupation of the heart with needs, and petitions are prayers of requests to God. After a time of intense communion, it almost seems mundane to present petitions to God, but He has invited us to do so.

In my own experience, even though I feel somewhat apologetic, I say, "Lord, I do have a few requests to make." So I present my petitions to Him. It is a good idea for every Christian to have a prayer list, so that when we present our petitions, we can do it in an orderly manner, but not in a structured or mechanical way. The Apostle Paul exhorts us, "Be anxious for nothing, but in everything by prayer and supplication with thanksgiving let your requests be made known to God. And the peace of God, which surpasses all comprehension, shall guard your hearts and your minds in Christ Jesus" (Philippians 4:6, 7).

Step Twelve:
A Remembrance and a Reminder

The final step is suggested by Ignatius of Loyola. In speaking about his times of communion with God, he asked, "After you have visited a flower garden and are getting ready to leave its beauty, what is the irresistible impulse that you have?" He answers his own question, "Why, it is to pick a flower, to take some of the fragrance of the garden with us."

As we pick that flower, taking its fragrance with us, we are reminded of our time in the beautiful flower garden; it serves as a remembrance of the beauty we saw; and it shows others where we have been.

As we conclude our time alone with God, the final step is to select the most refreshing part of our time of communion and fix it so firmly in our minds and affections that we will remember it throughout the day. It will serve as a reminder of our time with God. As the person who has been to the flower garden shows evidence that he has been there by the flower he has picked and taken with him, so our time in communion with the living God should remain fragrant to us and to all those whom we shall meet throughout the day.

Summary and Conclusion

In addition to having exercised the first aspect of the taproot of the soul in meditation, we now have seen how to share Christ's life by exercising the affections in communion. This prepares us for the final exercise of the taproot of the soul—choosing and obedience.

As we have learned to meditate in the Word of God night and day (Joshua 1:8; Psalm 1:2), so now we have learned how to have communion with Him, not just as one morning period of time—the quiet time—but as extending also throughout the day by means of reflection. The quiet time is but the first of many daily periods of communion. In addition to the practice exemplified by David (Psalm 55:17) and practiced by Daniel (Daniel 6:10), which is the spending of time with the Lord at morning, noon and evening, we can do more than "send up a word" now and then. It can be a refreshing experience to take a few seconds as many times as the routine of the day allows, and as a reflection, remembrance and reminder of the morning time spent with Him to tell Him . . .

- that He is on the throne
- that you thank Him for sending Jesus Christ to take away your sins
- that you love Him
- that He is very great
- that He has proven real to you
- that you praise Him for who He is
- that you praise Him for all that He has done
- that you choose to let Him be real to you in that moment in which you are right now and in those ahead.

Such experiences open the door to sharing Christ's life and having Him share yours. It is His method of watering your soul regardless of time, place or circumstances.

6

THE WILL IN CHOOSING
AND OBEDIENCE

Our God is intensely practical. Though time spent in meditation and communion will give us spiritual sensitivity, God knows that our real failures and successes are in the daily battles of life. We have looked at two parts of the taproot of the soul through which we share the life of Christ—the mind in meditation, the affections in communion. If we make a comparative size of the branches of the taproot, the one we will now consider is the largest—*the will in choosing*. God has arranged that the largest channel for sharing His life is available during the time that we need it most.

Much of our day consists of the affairs of life that are spent apart from conscious meditation and communion. And that remaining part of life (a large chunk of it, see Figure 2, page 41, the white section) is made up of a succession of choices. In these our wills are exercised. Now this is not an inferior part of the day's routine; it is very important to God, and He has made provision for us to be watered through that aspect of the taproot of the soul. The following illustration will help in bringing out the important point we now wish to make.

Prior to the entry of the United States into World War II, the German battleship *Graf Spee* was effectively raiding Allied ships in the South Atlantic. The British High Command assigned three cruisers, HMS *Exeter,* HMS *Achilles* and HMS *Ajax,* to the specific mission of intercepting and destroying the German raider. Commodore Harwood was in command of the operation. (As I relate this incident, I'm going to stick to the facts up to a point and then I'm going to depart from them; the point of departure will be obvious, and then we will make our application.) As the time for making the attack on the *Graf Spee* drew near, Commodore Harwood called the commanding officers of the three ships to his cabin on the flagship for a conference. He explained exactly what the strategy was and what was expected of each ship's crew. The briefing was completed and each captain understood what his part in the battle was to be. Commodore Harwood said, "All right, Gentlemen, let's go out and do our duty."

At this point, one of the three captains said, "Commodore, it was really great to have this time and conversation with you. The refreshments you served were really delightful. Your quarters are so enjoyable. The coffee and tea your steward served was first rate. Most of all, you're really a great person and it's really a privilege to spend time with you. Why do we have to go back to the battle? Why can't we just stay around and enjoy your company from now on? Let's forget about the nasty old war."

Should such an extraordinary request have been made, the Commodore's reply would have been something along these lines, "I'm glad you enjoyed the time we had; it was a delight to me also. Your idea of spending all of our time in fellowship is jolly good. As soon as the last battle has been fought and the last victory won, we'll have time enough for this kind of pleasure. Right now, Gentlemen, I'm more interested in what you do in the battle than I am in your time with me. Get the enemy in your sights. Remember I'm looking over your shoulder. All my resources are at your disposal. As you see the need for my advice, power or guidance, I'm as near as you can breathe the communication. I'll be watching and giving you directions even before you anticipate your need of me. Now, into battle!"

Though meditation in the Word of God and communion with God are very important, the battle of life is a priority. It is in this battle that our wills are exercised, and in which we have the privilege of sharing Christ's life as well as in meditation and communion.

Two Laws

In the daily warfare, certain laws are continually in action. Two of these are given by the Apostle Paul, "The law of the Spirit of life in Christ Jesus has set you free from the law of sin and of death" (Romans 8:2). To understand these laws—the law of the Spirit of life and the law of sin and of death—an appropriate illustration is to consider an airplane before taking off and while in flight.

Suppose you are about to take an airplane trip. The passengers are aboard with seatbelts fastened, and the plane taxis to the end of the runway. There is a delay. You wonder what communications are passing between the pilot and the control tower. At one time I imagined the pilot was saying to the tower operator, "The pull of gravity is still too strong for me to take off. What can you do to counteract it? Keep moving those levers and switches till you get gravity down to zero so it won't hold my plane down." This isn't exactly the case, of course, but gravity is holding the plane down.

After clearance has been given to the pilot, he roars down the runway. Soon he has gained flying speed and the plane is airborne. The law of gravity no longer controls the plane. A higher law has come into operation. Because of the shape of the wing and certain other factors, including forward motion, the law of gravity is effectively counteracted by a higher law. The law of aerodynamics has taken control.

Summarized, the factor which enabled the law of gravity to be overcome and the plane to be brought under the control of a higher law was forward motion. As long as forward motion is maintained, the plane will remain airborne. This is the principle for the victorious Christian life.

Figure 4

The accompanying diagram represents the profile of a plane in flight (Figure 4, above). We notice that the airplane is either climbing, flying level or descending. The diagram may also be a profile of our Christian life. We are either making progress, we're level or we're declining.

Every change in spiritual altitude is the result of a deliberate choice of the will. Joshua placed great importance on the will when he said, "Choose you this day whom ye will serve; . . . but as for me and my house, we will serve the Lord" (Joshua 24:15, KJV). Jesus Christ commended Mary in saying that she had *chosen* that right thing, "Only a few things are necessary, really only one, for Mary has chosen the good part" (Luke 10:42). All of us assume that when we are abiding in Christ, we are going along at a level segment in our spiritual lives. God sees that we have a need of nourishment, so He arranges circumstances in order that we may partake of His life. He allows temptation to come into our lives, even while we are abiding in Christ. In fact, James tells us to regard temptations as friends (James 1:2, PH), and indeed they are, because they allow us to appropriate Christ's life. Paul assures us that God will not allow us to be tempted beyond our ability to resist, but will with the temptations also provide a way out (see I Corinthians 10:13).

Choices in Temptation

In every public building there are lighted signs indicating exits by which a person may leave the building. Generally, these are alternate ways to the one by which he entered the building. He is never totally surrounded by closed doors. It is the same in our Christian lives; no matter how much we feel we are surrounded by temptations, God has placed exits there. So, as temptations come and we make the right choices, we feel good inside; we feel clean and happy. We advance in spiritual altitude. On the other hand, if we make a wrong decision, we start into a spiritual decline. This continues till we recognize we've made the wrong choice, confess it, make the right choice, and then resume climbing to a new spiritual altitude. And because we're human, we do make wrong choices.

Why do we make these wrong choices, which give us so much grief and heavy-heartedness? We do have an answer, but behind the explanation there is a principle that we must understand. Let us look closely at an illustration from Jesus' preaching when He said, "Whoever shall force you to go one mile, go with him two" (Matthew 5:41).

This statement may have been directed to first-century Christians who desired to witness to Roman soldiers who were so numerous throughout the empire. In those days, Roman soldiers not only had to walk most everyplace they went, but they had to carry heavy packs on their backs. Recognizing that this was a hardship, Roman law allowed any Roman soldier to commandeer a civilian and have him carry his pack from one milestone to the next. If the civilian refused, he could be prosecuted under Roman law. But having reached the milestone, the civilian had no further obligation. If the soldier tried to force him to carry his pack farther, the soldier could then be prosecuted under the same Roman law.

So Christ's admonition was, "When you've carried the pack to the next milestone, then *volunteer* for a second mile. Nobody has ever done that before for a Roman soldier. He'll wonder what makes you different. You can then share My love with him."

Using this same illustration, let us reverse and amplify it to try to answer the question as to why we make wrong choices. The passage we want to begin with is Paul's declaration, "Even so consider yourselves to be dead to sin" (Romans 6:11a).

Let's suppose that you were living in the days of the Roman soldier we have just described. You have to walk three miles to work every morning. One day, shortly after you appear on the highway going to work, a soldier overtakes you and hands you his pack. You gladly carry it to the next milestone. But when you reach the next milestone, the soldier looks around, sees that no one is nearby, and says, "Sorry, buddy, you'll have to carry it on down the road." You tell him that the law says that you don't have to carry it and that you're invoking the law in your own behalf.

The soldier then rolls up his sleeves, shows his large muscles and puts one hand on his double-edged sword. With threatening and browbeating, he says, "You're going to carry it to the next milestone or else!" Considering his size, threats and aggressiveness, what would you do? You'd probably carry the pack to the next milestone.

Now if this went on day after day, you would certainly look for a solution. You would look around the complex where you worked and perhaps find a senior officer in the Roman army, a judge who held court in the complex, a policeman, and several friends amply equipped with large muscles. Then you would ask them to meet you at the second milestone the following morning.

The same scenario would again be repeated. You would say to the soldier, "The law says I don't have to carry your pack beyond this milestone, and I'm invoking the law." As he started his threatening, you would call your friends over.

You'd say to the officer, "Does a soldier have the right to do this?"

He would reply, "No."

You would ask the judge if this law had been tested in court.

He would say it had, and it was a valid law.

You'd ask the policeman if he was going to enforce the law.

And he'd answer, "Yes."

For good measure, you'd call on your friends with the muscles and ask if they would help out, and they would assure you that they would.

You have been able to invoke the law because of the resources you were able to call up. Paul's statement (Romans 6:11) has given some people more problems than help. That's because they generally read only the first part of the verse, "Consider yourselves to be dead to sin." They've left out the second part, "But alive to God in Christ Jesus" (Romans 6:11b).

We can invoke the fact that we're dead to the law only as we call on the resources. We are dead to the obligation to sin, but not to the inclination to sin. When we make a wrong choice, it's because we have forgotten to call up the resources God has made available. When this happens, David reminds us, "The steps of good men are directed by the Lord. He delights in each step they take. If they fall it isn't fatal, for the Lord holds them with His hand" (Psalm 37:23, 24, LB).

Complete Forgiveness

A wrong choice is never fatal for Christians. The directions God gives in His Word are most familiar, "If we confess our sins, He is faithful and righteous to forgive us our sins and to cleanse us from all unrighteousness" (I John 1:9). Solomon said, "He who conceals his transgressions will not prosper, but he who confesses and forsakes them will find compassion" (Proverbs 28:13).

I heard of an incident in which a penitent was confessing his wrongdoings. In the process he said, "I want to confess that I stole some hay from my neighbor."

The one to whom he was confessing instructed, "Be more specific. How much did you steal?"

The penitent said, "I stole half a load, but make it a whole load. I'm going to get the other half tonight."

This seems to be a negative illustration of what it means not only to confess, but to forsake. As long as we have the intention of repeating the sin, we have not confessed and forsaken it. As we confess and volitionally forsake the intent to ever repeat the wrong choice, God's multidimensional forgiveness comes into play. A song has put several Scriptures together:

> As far as east is from the west,
> And deep as the deepest sea,
> Behind God's back and blotted out,
> Christ moved my sins from me.

David spoke these wonderful words, "As far as the east is from the west, so far has He removed our transgressions from us" (Psalm 103:12). If you were to take off in a long-range airplane from an airport which had an east-west runway, and would fly west all the way around the world and land on the same runway, you would still be going west when you landed, never having gone east. If you would take off on the same runway going east, fly all the way around the world and land on the same runway, you would still be going east when you landed, never having gone west. But if you took off on a north-south runway and went around the world, every time you reached the north or south poles, you would change directions. The distance between the poles is measurable, but there is no way of measuring the distance between east and west—they do not exist in the same dimension.

When God says He's removed our sins as far from us as the east is from the west, this is multi-dimensional forgiveness. Paul uses some great words in his letter to the Romans. One of them is the word *propitiation* (Romans 3:25). It means that there's no charge pending against any Christian in any court in heaven. Another great word is *justification* (Romans 3:28; 4:25; 5:1). It seems to correspond with, "Their sins and their lawless deeds I will remember no more" (Hebrews 10:17). Through justification we understand that God has not only blotted out the fact of our sins from His memory, but He has blotted them out of the pages of history.

Someone has said, "God cannot change history." But He seems to have where the forgetting of sin is concerned. Scripture states that it was 480 years from the time the children of Israel came out of Egypt to the fourth year of Solomon, when he began to build the house of the Lord (I Kings 6:1). If we compute that the children of Israel spent 40 years in the wilderness, took 20 years under

Joshua to conquer Canaan, were under the judges for 450 years (Acts 13:20), that Saul reigned 40 years and David 40 years, and it was the fourth year of Solomon's reign in which the building of the temple was begun, we have then a total of not 480 years, but 594 years.

One historian has computed that the periods of disobedience during the time of the judges totals 114 years, the exact amount of the "discrepancy." The sons of Korah stated, "Thou didst forgive the iniquity of Thy people. Thou didst cover all their sin" (Psalm 85:2). Assuming this explanation is valid, God computes the period of time from the Exodus till the beginning of the building of the temple as 480 years, even though the historian says it was 594 years. When God wants something out of His memory, He blocks it out of the record of history.

Justification means that God has not only blotted out the memory of our sins from His memory, but He's blotted them out of the records of history. There is no excuse for us to be nursing a wounded ego after we have sinned, but rather we are to confess, volitionally forsake and get on back into the battle of life. Just as we exercised the will improperly in making the wrong choice, we now exercise it properly in confessing and getting on with the struggles of life in which there is no furlough (see Ecclesiastes 8:8).

Conscious Choosing

Referring back to our diagram, (Figure 4, page 82), each change of an airplane's altitude is a result of alternating control by the law of gravity or the law of aerodynamics.

In the Christian life each change of spiritual altitude is the result of a conscious or barely conscious *choice* by the will. When we make the right decision in time of temptation, we then feel right in our hearts. David declared, "Trust in the Lord, and do good; so shalt thou dwell in the land, and verily thou shalt be fed" (Psalm 37:3, KJV). In New Testament language, he was saying, "Choose good or choose right and your soul will be fed— your soul will be fully watered by Christ's life." The evolution of temptation usually follows this pattern: first, suggestion, second, consideration and third, decision. As long as the will has not made its decision, the suggestion or even the consideration of a sin is not defiling. But when we *make* the decision—yes or no—it is then that we have sinned or we have won the victory. When we make the right decision in temptation, we share Christ's life and our souls are fed. And this happens constantly in our daily lives. We're faced with many temptations. We have the opportunity to share Christ's life as we think about the right choices just as we do in meditation and in communion.

The Lord graciously provides many opportunities to do His will and consequently to experience having our souls watered by Him. Isaiah records God's promise: "If you give yourself to the hungry, and satisfy the desire of the afflicted, then your light will rise in darkness, and your gloom will become like midday. And the

Lord will continually guide you, and satisfy your desire in scorched places, and give strength to your bones; and you will be like a watered garden, and like a spring of water whose waters do not fail" (Isaiah 58:10, 11). In our daily walk we're told that if we draw out our souls to the hungry and satisfy those who are afflicted, God will water us with His life. We will be able actually to share His life. To accomplish this, God places needy people in our paths.

These may be Christians who need to be ministered to, or non-Christians who need the message of salvation. As we are given these opportunities, we share Christ's life by making the right decisions. When we pour out our souls to the needy, we are answered that "he who waters will himself be watered" (Proverbs 11:25). So as we pour ourselves out to others, our souls are in turn watered.

But not all of the Christian life is responding to what we are supposed to do in temptation or in pouring out our lives to the needy, Christian and non-Christian alike. The Christian life is not just rising or declining—it is also "flying" level. That aspect of it may be called abiding. It is possible to spend hours with someone—someone you love— and not even speak a word; but as long as nothing has happened to interrupt our fellowship, then we are abiding—spending time in each other's presence, "flying" at an even keel. Thus all day long we are either ascending, abiding or descending.

An interesting portrayal of this truth may be

seen in one of the songs of ascent. The psalmist states, "Behold, as the eyes of servants look to the hand of their master, as the eyes of a maid to the hand of her mistress; so our eyes look to the Lord our God, until He shall be gracious to us" (Psalm 123:2). The setting of this psalm seems to be an Oriental banquet. The hostess, unseen by her guests, is in the line of sight of maids who have been trained from their early years to watch the hand of their mistress. This is the reason they are called *hand*maidens. As the meal progresses, the hostess notes that one of the guests needs a glass of water, another a piece of bread, another butter, and she gives a very subtle hand signal. So subtle, in fact, that a baseball scout would probably not even be able to pick it up. As the nearest handmaiden sees the signal, she responds, and the need of the guest is met. Now, what would happen if the maid's eye wandered? Someone's need would go unmet. In the same way, we need to be on the alert to get the necessary signals from God; directions on what we're to do in temptation, and what we're to do in pouring out our lives to the Christian and non-Christian alike.

During British naval maneuvers, involving a column of cruisers, a signal was given to execute a 90-degree turn. The maneuver was performed, except for one cruiser whose captain missed the turn signal. It almost collided with the one ahead of it. The formation was totally disrupted. By skillful seamanship, the captains of the remaining cruisers kept clear of the offending ship. When the commotion finally settled down, the admiral in command sent an urgent signal to the offending captain, "Captain, what is your intention?"

The cruiser captain, having reflected on what his inattention cost him in his naval career, replied, "Sir, my intention is to buy a farm." Because he had missed just one signal, his reputation for skillfulness in warfare was in serious question, and his career was prematurely ended.

We develop skill in spiritual warfare by being alert to the Holy Spirit's signals. Thus we prevail over our spiritual enemies. We choose by an act of the will to obey God—in resisting temptation and in pouring out our souls to the hungry. God responds to that kind of commitment by flooding our souls with His divine watering, as we exercise our wills in choosing to obey Him.

SUMMARY AND CONCLUSION

In the previous chapters we have considered God's provision for our souls to take root downward and bear fruit upward. We have looked at promises from the Word of God that our souls would be watered, and we would share Christ's life as we exercise our minds in meditation, our affections in communion and our wills in choosing and obeying.

Is that all that is required, then, for successful Christian living? You no doubt have observed in your own experience that it is quite possible to spend time meditating in God's Word, communing with Him and following Him obediently, yet to react to unanticipated situations in a non-Christlike manner. An unresolved problem seems to remain.

A comparison of spiritual and physical reactions will help us get to the root of that problem and find its solution. We have five senses which seem to be contending perpetually for our bodies' responses. Once we have felt the softness of a newborn baby's cheek, we are drawn almost irresistibly to *touch* it again. In visiting a flower garden our sense of *smell* is tantalized by the fragrance of our favorite odor. If we are connoisseurs of excellent foods, our *taste* buds direct us to our favorite gastronomic delicacies. If we are trained to appreciate fine music, we find that in the midst of a variety of sounds, our ears are drawn to that melody with which our *hearing* harmonizes. In the presence of many beautiful colors, how irresistibly our *sight* is fastened on the royal color of gold. Our five senses are representative of many voices which compete for our complete response and attention.

In a similar manner, there are many voices in our hearts clamoring for our souls' attentions. Paul lists quite a number of these: "Immorality, impurity, sensuality, idolatry, sorcery, enmities, strife, jealousy, outbursts of anger, disputes, dissensions, factions, envyings, drunkenness, carousings, and things like these" (Galatians 5:19-21).

In unplanned circumstances we generally respond to the voice we have cultivated most diligently. It ought to be the voice of the Holy Spirit of God, not speaking audibly, of course, but through a definite impression on our hearts and minds that have been saturated by the Word of God.

The most treacherous of the competing voices is that of self. When we feed our egos on self-pity, blame, criticism of others and in choosing to indulge what the Church Fathers called the seven deadly sins—pride, envy, anger, covetousness, gluttony, lust, sloth—we strengthen the voices which may well overpower the Holy Spirit's in a time of crisis.

God's command in such a situation is this: "Mortify therefore your members which are upon the earth . . . [and Paul lists another set of 'voices']" (Colossians 3:5, KJV).

These voices are not necessarily silenced by a lifted hand in a meeting, throwing a fagot on the fire at camp or by the finality of a single decision. Rather, they are starved into insensibility by disuse. As we exercise the positive, the negative diminishes in strength. So as we nourish our souls in meditation, communion and right choices and obeying, we respond to Christ and are strengthening our sensitivities to hear the inner voice of God.

As we nourish these powers and deny the dissenting voices, we are growing toward maturity and the fuller enjoyment of Jesus Christ. We become increasingly like the fruit-bearing tree which never ceases to yield fruit, regardless of the time, place or circumstances.